THE PEEPSHOW GIRL

July 1989

MARION LOMAX

The Peepshow Girl

For Sue,
with love,
Marion

BLOODAXE BOOKS

ISBN: 1 85224 072 5

First published 1989 by
Bloodaxe Books Ltd,
P.O. Box 1SN,
Newcastle upon Tyne NE99 1SN.

Bloodaxe Books Ltd acknowledges
the financial assistance of Northern Arts.

Typesetting by Bryan Williamson, Manchester.

Printed in Great Britain by
Billings & Son Limited, Worcester.

For my mother,
Margaret Bolam

Acknowledgements

Acknowledgements are due to the editors of the following publications in which some of these poems first appeared: *A Royal Audience* (Berkshire County Library, 1985), *Alternative Poetry: Counter-currents* (Winchester School of Art, 1984), *Dilettante* (Reading University), *The Gregory Awards Anthology 1981 & 1982* (Carcanet/Society of Authors, 1982), *The Literary Review, London Magazine, The Month in Yorkshire, Outposts, Poetry Durham, Poetry Review, Slipping Glimpses* (Poetry Book Society Supplement, Winter 1985), *Strawberry Fare, The Telegraph Sunday Magazine, The Times Literary Supplement, Writing Women,* and *York Arts Centre Poetry Anthology* (1981).

'Passengers' was broadcast on *Poetry Now* (BBC Radio 3). 'The Forked Tree' was a first prize winning poem in the 1981 Cheltenham Festival Poetry Competition.

Some of these poems were included in a collection for which Marion Lomax received an Eric Gregory Award in 1981.

Cover painting: *Going Out: 27.10.1981* by Avigdor Arikha. Oil on canvas, 81 x 64.8 cm (Jerusalem, Israel Museum).

Contents

On Independence and Resolution

THE FORKED TREE

Photographer's Model

He needed a girl for an afternoon
To sit pretty, sporting a straw hat.
He said: You'll be a pin-up in Clapham
Between racks of ethnic skirts and dresses.

You've a natural look, no cosmetics,
No city smile – just what the store ordered.
I resented that store picking on me
Making my gaucherie fit its requirements.

But the challenge seduced me and I went
To the studio to see the straw hat
And sit pretty in front of his new lens
And a wall of huge breasts with city smiles.

Turn this way. It was hot under the lights.
Look up. Look back. The hat began to wilt.
Head to the side. Right. Now bring your eyes back.
It has to look natural. Concentrate.

I wondered how long he had had to wait
For the breasts to swing into city smiles.
He laughed. Cities have their natural sides –
His camera whirred in the undergrowth.

Laburnum

Another year and the laburnum drips
Beneath the bedroom balcony. Outside
I stand to watch the windows fill and clear.
My legs won't move, but I have no desire
To stand at the foot of your bed, or meet
You on your way downstairs to sit with her –
Reading your tea-leaves as you check the lawn
For murderous cats who track daffodils
And dislocate their necks, as you did mine.
Spring is a dangerous time. You reach out
For toast and marmalade. Shredded lemon
Sprawling nervously in jelly, trembles
At the probing of your knife. She yawns quite
Unaware. Folds the newspaper down at
The local page. Sighs, 'Nothing happens here,'
And you answer – 'Ah, but it will my dear.'

Another year and the laburnum seeds
Hurl themselves past the bedroom balcony.
I watch you move through the surgery and
Wash your hands. You manipulate bones like
The expert you are. The women unbend:
Open. Close. Beneath your sinuous hands.
You brush the tell-tale petals from the couch.
Seeds fall past the glass: you draw the curtain.
If the cat who tracked down the daffodils
Swallowed these seeds and died, it would be a
Surrogate death. No one can suspect that
I am alive; nor will they guess why you
Should give her a green dress. With her dark hair
You will need to be more inventive. She
May not leave her body as readily
As I embraced the colours of this tree.

Willow Pattern

The rustle and tap of a green-feathered bird
On the bars of its bamboo pagoda cage
Creep into the thoughts of the new-wedded girl
As she watches the leaves fall, combing her hair.

Last summer she lay overlooking a lake
Leaf shadows on pillows: her lover asleep.
Cobwebs at open windows filtered their breath
Through the secretive willows and the small bridge.

The green bird is changing: its feathers ring down.
For weeks now she has not cleaned the cage, but sits
Listening for the rustle of willow in wind –
His tap at the door: their feet pounding the bridge.

Portrait

She protects him from patrons' painted smiles.
'I will not *have* women' – his brush is poised,
'They trap mosquitoes between their skirts:
My room is inviolate, but for you.'
She shrugs, 'Perhaps if you have a moment
This afternoon – the children are asleep...'

As she leaves, he slides the door into place
Her face on wood – serene, unreproaching:
The one he painted to be sure of it.

He works in oils which take days to dry;
She steers the children out of his wake,
Spends hours alone with the creak of boats,
Babies crawling over varnished floors,
And the pastel evenings when she sews.

He will stay in the studio till first light.
Like Mariana, she stands looking out –
The mosquitoes war-dance on the water:
Wheat lodges in the fields every night.

The Other Woman

She chooses her clothes in subdued colours
To suit a life rehearsed in the suburbs.
She rarely needs to appear in public –
Has no one to take her to the opera
Or out to a restaurant in the evening
While someone minds legitimate children.

His avenue paths are hung with lilac
Proud candles erect on the horse-chestnut
Laburnum dangling her gaudy earrings
Over into other people's gardens.
He has never dared to send her roses:
She buys herself flowers from street corners.

He comes to her flat while it is still light
And makes her curtain off the afternoon
So even then, she hardly sees his face.
Each week their liaison seems more unreal:
She raises her veil, the netted window –
Sees him vanish at the end of the street.

Recurrent Dream

I park my car in your cul-de-sac, walk past
The fronts of houses opening onto the path.
A crowd of people are gathered at your door –
All women. I can't see your expression, yet
I know you are the figure in the doorway
Because one by one they level squat black guns
Below your left shoulder. My mind is racing.
I leave the pin in a grenade and hurl it.
They scatter without taking aim. Relieved
I run to find your door is closed against me –
Another woman's voice scolding you within.

Signifier and Signified

Tulips does have something
Of the flower in it –
The *u* opening its lips
l of leaves uncurling.

Even the sound fits their
Sensuous chaste creaking
As they so slowly bend.

I still don't know myself
Well enough to see if
My name looks like me: I
Stare at the letter *M*.

Your label is short, not
At all like you. Two vowels
Merge and fall to softness.

The last stiff consonant
Is hard and final, which
Is the way I know you –
Open and closed letters.

It begins to go back

There is no trace of you
In the quiet room: even the light
Fades – has moved across the fields,
Glows now on the corner of the hill:
It begins to go back.

Your train pulled out an hour ago;
At this moment you reach Victoria.
As I straighten the cover on the bed
And the birds say all there is to be said –
It begins to go back.

You merge with the crowds:
My lost perfume diminishes with the afternoon;
The traffic parts five different ways.
You follow the roads to Lambeth Bridge
And cross the river with the wind.

Fifty miles upstream
We walked it down with dragonflies
And a lame swan.
This water which, without a sound,
Passes now, shares only time
Of coexistence and moves on
As you have done – while I
Read in the silent room
The poem I found before you came.
The cats return to wait and sit;
Apples drop – the clock does not tick:
It begins to go back.

Les Passe-Roses

The hollyhocks have grown ambitious.
Risking top rungs, their flowers open
To swing soft bells with stiff gold clappers;
The bees hum as if they had just rung
A moment ago: their colours clash.

Sparrows seduce them with gutter songs;
Shake out bees in a rustle of silk.
Their bonnets slip – the long afternoon
Loosens as they let it go, while we
Smile and strive to hold a youthful pose.

As summer passes they come of age
In a long inexpert chorus-line,
Kicking high their flimsy camisoles –
Dance themselves out with an abandon
That women envy as they grow old.

Tenement Haiku

In a spacious room
A girl plays a violin
Rephrasing her youth.

The women work on
Straining to hear a distant
And difficult tune.

Passengers

An old woman sifts through sepia prints,
Photographs and faded postcards –
Regards a picture of herself as a girl
Sitting stiff-backed in an Edwardian hat.
The curve of her cheek, flawless skin,
Lips pertly pressed, and the profile
Of her breasts beneath those crisp pleats,
That tight bodice and high neck.

Moving back behind the glass
Into the insect-laden dusk
Her skirt sweeps the veranda steps.
Babies sleep under mosquito nets
The rockers scrape; she hears the veld
Softly dousing the sunbird's breast
And as her lips remember it
She tips the starlings' wings with red.

Day brings the boy with a pony and trap:
She clambers up – sets off alone.
Beneath her veil she feels the rain
Gather to obscure the view, as locusts did
That afternoon the sky went black.
Too soon, out here, the gullies fill
And wash you down: she cracks the whip.
A whistle sounds across the veld.

The day they came from Pietermaritzburg
He smoked with the guard and held her glove.
Now she rides the long mountain train
That twists like a snake and steeply turns
Till the room shudders to a wrinkled hand.
A bemused passenger, she rubs the glass
Of the last carriage; looking back –
At herself, staring forward in the first.

Magnolia Tree

Blood-stemmed, the pink buds grow in pairs of claws.
Burying their hardness in a deep sky,
They span into light feathers, plucked upright.

Last spring another woman watched the sight.
Stood at this window, moved throughout the house
Pursued by rain; the pale shadow of wings.

Out there a bird, which she used to feed, sings
For me – forgetful of her kindnesses.
Notes which would have quelled her panicking fear.

Sometimes, at dusk, I think she might appear
Quietly – to watch the claws of her pain
Soften – as they did, into feathers; rain.

Roots

Some nights I hear them digging in the foundations.
The whole house echoes with the tap of roots
Feeling their way in the darkness
Trying to get in.
They follow me from place to place
Refusing to be jilted
Scratching more desperately with each new move.
Perhaps they break through into the scarred
Neutral rooms when I have gone.

I dare not yield to their sinewy arms
But they haunt me after dark like dead lovers.
Too frequently old curtains open on new scenes
Never again to have that relationship
With a field of sunflowers
Or the hill scattered with beehives
Or wake to find the farm lying beside me.
Instead I flirt briefly with new cracks in the ceiling
And have promiscuous affairs with a variety of views.

Last night they reached this house and I heard them.
Leaving my bed I went down, took a pick,
Smashed through the floorboards; only mandrakes
Grew between the joists, silently sucking the earth,
Feeding on what had drained there.
I pulled them frantically, smothered each one –
Buried the misshapen children end to end
In a drawer by the bed. Then I closed it
On a harvest of stilled screams, and slept.

The Father's Story: a Pre-Raphaelite Dream

The lamps were flat white lilies in my sorrow.
The window, tree, and curtain made a painting.
Inside her cot she waited for an angel;
A polished tile – the pool of light was empty.
Mary, your name could not have graced our daughter:
Her place was usurped by a ghostly sister.

Christina. Stand-in, like Rossetti's sister.
A silent child whose face meant only sorrow,
Who never heard or knew the name of daughter,
Who lay so still and lifeless like a painting
Draining my heart until it was quite empty
And I the victim of an evil angel.

Rossetti knew there should have been an angel.
Just like the one appearing to his sister.
A girl to make the void no longer empty.
A single tree for Paradise and Sorrow:
Eden. Golgotha. In a window painting.
A fragile thing of glass and blood, my daughter.

Only a splintered dream, this icon daughter
Who should have grown to be a living angel,
A painted heroine who left her painting
To run and play with those calling her sister;
Now locked unborn inside their mother's sorrow
To curse her damaged womb, forever empty.

At last I journeyed where the fields were empty
To paint a red bird swooping to my daughter.
The light had to be right to catch the sorrow.
Circling the skies a predatory angel.
The river took her down to meet her sister:
I buried them together in my painting.

Her small life floats there still within this painting,
Spread out with grass and flowers, her face empty.
I carry it for all of them – each sister
They feared might be a changeling like my daughter.
The whole tribe can feel safe because an angel
Has exorcised their fears and killed his sorrow.

Goat-like in sorrow, my dead eyes are empty.
A sea of painting swallows up my daughter.
A lonely angel on a beach calls 'Sister'.

Her husband speaks to her of Dragons

Haruko, I give up my mind to you
To swell whatever space you now inhabit:
It swirls with the dragons of your silk kimono
Dipped in violence the dark cannot articulate.
Our daughter wrestles with it in the night
We both keep echoes to soothe such spasms –
Sometimes she starts, listens, as if your voice
Is being rung across the fields, calling her to sleep.
In the morning she wakes dry-eyed: I weep.

Your grandfather's sword still hangs where it did.
I will shame both our families if I cannot heal
This sickness of wanting what is denied.
On the door your empty clothes-hanger strikes
Your absence – one, two (softly), three...four.
It is not the goldfinches' glass song
Or that high plaintive music of your own
As you smoothed hair under tall combs –
But the stubborn rejection of wire by wood.

I have laid away everything you wore:
Even the familiar has grown hard,
Oppressing me with trivialities made cruel.
Help me to kill my desire, to think of you
As one who found a better love elsewhere.
Let me find a clue that you had plans
To be more than a mother and my wife.
If I thought you safe I could forgive
Even the base charade of death.

I need to know that this was ordained;
That like the branches of the cherry, you reach up
And are not lost in earth to a stale faith.
This girl here has your eyes, but not your soul:
She comforts and torments me with your smile.
We meet through her – for her sake, it must cease.
We must not let her stumble from our bed
To her own low mattress, flanked by dragons –
Lips set under the weight of your clothes.

Blencathra

The sky is like nothing else in the garden
Cornflower, delphinium, nor campanula.
Spokes of lavender wheel it round. I sit here
So pain can watch it seed clouds, tease them out
Into faces which start to say something
Then dissolve. It forms mountains on air
Supporting each other: a balance of vapour.
It has walled in the world with a hard blue –
No gaps. Clouds to the fore, it slides past slowly
An unbroken belt. We rest against it
Moving closer: night tightens its notch.

As a child, when relatives died, I searched
For their features in the clouds. Not long ago
My father smiled above Blencathra. You say
You cannot bear to lose me to the weather.
My love, I would stay up here forever, where
An invisible tide turns in the trees,
Church bells are silent in the valley and shreds
Of tattered rope float out like hands through
The slatted tower: time must be slower.
Streams flow down the mountain; somewhere
An old glacier is still coldly melting.

In this high place the sky has quiet power –
Strolling through the house opening up windows.
My face pressed to the landscape of your chest
We share an internal world of stars – when I ache
You bury me under a weight of sky to wake smiling.
Other nights my features vaporise, look down
On you, alone in a borrowed garden,
Where the sky supported our sheltered dreams.
The city forces us to speak less, think more –
Restless against a blue, paler than eyes,
Wearied by hoardings that never stop talking.

The Forked Tree

I killed two hares last night in the heart of the garden.
Long ears in moonlight, mimicking the shape of the tree.
I crept round the side of the house before they sensed me
And when they heard the gun clear its throat it was too late.
I hit the buck first, then the doe – stupidly standing
To stare at me. Her powerful hindquarters refusing
To kick and run, though I knew she could have bounded up
The lane in an instant, back to her young. I can cope
With hares: they are easy to cook. I feel no remorse.
Now I'll wait for the vixen who raids the chicken house.

I feed my chickens. Gather and sort the eggs. I wipe
The dirt and straw collage from the shells of those I sell.
I have the dogs too. My husband trained them, but I was
Surprised how quickly they obeyed me. I talked to them –
More easily than I talked to the children. Could share
The shadow with its dark gun lurking by our house wall
And the silent bullet lodged inside before we knew
That it was growing. His coming out of hospital,
Then the sniper's second strike when he was off his guard.
In the end I could only stand stupidly and stare –

Even with warning, could not believe such treachery.
The children were swinging from the tree in the garden
With no one to catch them. Darkness made the ground tremble
With hooves which left the grass trampled and the roses spoiled.
I guard this warren – small rooms and scattered outbuildings.
Not even chickens shall live in fear of predators.
My children shall feed better than before. Lonely nights
Are not without fear, but I cope with darkness now that
I have seen it bring young deer down from the wood to play.
Jumping in and out in the moonlight, through the forked tree.

LAST TRACES

Last Traces

Light stitches the trees
In tapestry. They
Gleam in bright cottons
Stretched taut on a frame.
A needle gathers
The valley up in
A pucker of green.

The embroidery grows
More lush each season:
The mill has to fight
Its way though branches.
Chimneys are bobbins
For fast-winding vines
From runaway looms.

These defiant ruins
Spin out the silence
Round gossiping birds
And a busy stream.
There are no machines;
No women's voices;
Few remnants remain.

But where clogs clattered
Towards their shuttles
In the needle light
The lane is woven
With exotic weeds
Which came with the cotton
And refused to leave.

Topsoil

I walk these moors for what they are.
The wind's runways. It swoops
Whoo-ing in my ears like sad owls,
Their beaks at my face where
The scarf can't cover. Beyond them
Curlews, constantly panicking,
Calling away from invisible nests.

This is the sky's full drop.
It doesn't have to cramp around cities
Or spear itself on spires.
Here it can stretch down its legs
And walk. It strides over the heather
Farther than I can see. The curlews
Call between its knees.

I walk these moors for what they are.
Neglected roof gardens of the mill towns
Left to fend for themselves, riding
The landscape with a small burden of sheep
And Sunday walkers. Where purple flowers
Tongue a late summer bell
Pealing low blue notes.

The marsh sucks my feet to a certain depth
And no further. The old sheep tracks lie
Deep down with monks' footprints.
Below, an Iron Age prospector once scratched
For ore, plundered trees for his furnace,
And below, a Bronze Age shepherd
Slept beneath them.

It matters little that the Vikings came
Or the Romans landed. That once this
Vast scar of heath was solid ice
Or fertile forest. The peat preserves
Old seeds: all swallowed now and
Well digested. I walk these moors
For what they are.

Unto this Last

the only book, properly to be called
a book, that I have ever yet written
myself, the one that will stand, (if
anything stand), surest and longest
of all work of mine.
                    JOHN RUSKIN

Last year's lambs are outcasts on bare hillsides:
No flocks move to market. In his valley
An empty dining room with ten places
Looks at the world through seven church windows
Of clear glass: one for each Gothic lamp lit
By high prose. A blue sail and a red ride
On the cold edge of air between mountains.
Black cattle carefully select the best grass.
I feel I should get better if only
I could lie down in Coniston water.

Paintings place him by a study window
Cabinet drawers standing open; same green chair –
His beard blotting each meticulous page.
Though he finished that chapter years ago
And someone cleared his papers from the floor,
Rearranged the books, sold a sketch or two,
Let the tourists come – we have not moved far.
For Turner-lined turrets, our new nightmares.
The rich found other wealth than life; the poor
Still have not enough to help each other.

Our times have moved back to an empty desk –
Dust spreads between us and the scenery:
He would not lie down in this Coniston.
His pen would not rest for men, nature, art –
Praised women as the angels of the house.
Of his age. Our prejudice is money.
The columns of St Mark's rise from nothing
To support an architectural heaven
In his drawing room. He bows over books,
A betrayed lake, these sails, a field of cows.

The Hag's Daughter

Behind the church a limestone well
Drips persistently on an old doll
Left long ago to be turned to stone
By her mother's so-called sorcery.

An old woman now, she has back-packed
Her hump between the houses
For eighty years. She never shared
Her mother's indifference to these people.

Still they turn away in the street.
Kindly enough, but reluctant to stand
Long in her gaze – as if afraid that
The sediment in her eyes may petrify.

Emily

I don't know how they dared
Put you under the pavement
In the family vault when
There was so much moor.

Even the graveyard is more
Akin, its strict boundaries
Holding back a silent
Clamour of escaped

Weeds and tangled flowers
Moving wildly in the wind.
You'd frown to see the crowds
Flocking to the house

Convinced they sense your spirit
In the reconstructed kitchen.
It's almost as naive
As those good churchmen

Believing that you'd let them
Tuck you safely into dust.
It suggests great folly, or
Even greater trust.

Second Wife

This house with a past is appropriate.
Each of us is new only to the other
We all lived with someone else
Before we finally came together.

You talk of years in empty rooms,
Of a garden – like this one – gone to seed.
Nettles and honeysuckle choking in turn;
Sharp-beaked birds nesting in the weed.

I gouge out roots and clear the stones.
Work hard, but grow disturbed to find –
Beneath the weeds a pattern shows
Which, earlier, someone else designed.

Just Another Commuter

Two seats in front: just out of reach
As the bus lurches on I stare
At his back and his old black jacket
Worn light in places, bagging with age.
I see the space where his workbag
Pressed his shoulder, and growing bolder
I look into the dark window
And try to see his face, but his neighbour
Is nearer and hides him from view.

From here he could well be my father,
But rather than make, what can only be
An embarrassing mistake, I sit until
We reach our destination. His thinning hair
Has one side brushed over;
I wonder if he will still know me –
Remembering him too well, I don't feel
So much older. We reach the terminus
And he is still too far to touch.

I know it is a futile hope – not having
Seen him for so long, but foolish thoughts
Haunt as we move down. He turns. One glance
Changes the familiar frame into a stranger.
I had always known it would be so, yet
Did not know which was the worst to bear –
The disappointment I felt at being left,
Or the relief at being spared
Seeing a dead man walk towards the stairs.

The Desk

It stood in the corner of the shop window
Carrying fifty-six inches of ship, aground
On its walnut surface, swirling with dust.
The four drawers on either side were false:
They swung open together like ships' lockers;
But the one in the centre was real and rasped
When it moved along a sanded slipway.
More than I could afford, but I bought it anyway,
And a man in a shabby jerkin removed the ship,
Casting the desk off without a cargo.

I anchored it between the shutters of this window.
The wasteland yaws between glass and sky.
Hands of red and green Virginia creeper
Reach wetly over the top of a wall.
It has rained ever since I left my old city;
The tide goes out through four lanes of traffic,
Beacons flashing at the end of the street.
The desk is loaded with papers, spilling over.
I float here charting a way to evening –
Leaving black lines in the wake of my pen.

The Lady of the House

Her sequins spoil me: the lamps remember –
Across the water, its face in its hands,
The big house was shuttered. Strings of horses
Side-stepping ramps: an indifferent drizzle.

She wore this dress the evening she came here
En route to America: a halter
Of old pearls swayed behind the gazebo.
Sometimes I know why my father loved her.

Last month he tried to recall her features,
How sun sprang the slope, sparking on roses;
Lit fires in the highly strung bone china
She would hold to her like an antique brooch.

I see an old woman in Oregon
With middle aged children – scanning the sea
From the wrong coast. Her wild mane of white hair
And soft mouth as determined as ever.

Finally parted, I have her letters;
One, from the week he died – undelivered.
The rest he reined up with crimson ribbon
In a trunk deep with her mildewed fine clothes.

Eurydice

Only a poet could mourn as you do
Bringing your music through the darkest gate
To plead for my return; have it granted.
Gentle Persephone wept, remembering.
Then you were clambering back to daylight
And I followed you up through the valleys
Of Avernus, dreaming of the meadows
And your soft pillow: our deserted bed.
We climbed in silence up the sloping path.
The darkness seemed to me to be singing
Its way to the surface, carrying us
With it. I did see the daylight before
You looked back, casting me into the depths.

It is harder to die the second time
But how could I blame you? It was only
Through love that you turned, fearing my stumbling:
Anxious, as I was, to be in your arms.
I will never complain of being loved.
It is the only lightness in this gloom –
To dream of bright shadows – the upper world
Where our marriage is a far-away house
I look back to sometimes with my veiled eyes;
Seeing you move from window to window.
But I fear you have stumbled many times
Distracting yourself from waiting for me,
Soothed by the empty beauty of young boys.

Her Last Request

Above Taurus and the Pleiades
A comet graces the same sky
She looked on then. I feel
I know her every glance,
The way her eyes turned to the west
As mine move northwards seeking you.
She speaks, 'Sleep now, so many leagues
Are spread between us.' Let me dream...

Night flowers kneel up in the borders
Wimpled women stride by the wall
As pigeons shrug rucked coats of mail
And I write dangerously to you
In a small book fastened by a chain
To this dark gown. Let me cast you
In the folds below my waist. Our names
Are nearer on a hundred tongues
Than we may ever be.

The two heart nightshade heralds truth:
There is silence in the ruin flower,
Belladonna. May you seem to come
When these arches swallow me.
I hear you in the hills
Above the lilies and still water
And your face moves nearer
As I sign this 'Guinevere'.

Isabelle of France

Ineluctable:
The rain drips
Like a clock
In this quiet house.

Love is a strange brooch —
I will grow old here
Among the fruit trees,
Mending my jewellery

Letting these eaves birds
Scrabble at my heart.
Butterflies, bruised flowers:
Stoical roses.

Light stirs the garden —
A foreign country.
No chance of meeting
Anyone I know.

The eloquent rain
Wakes me with stories,
Told through centuries
Of roses and snow.

A Jacobean Fragment

I am a dagger in
A dark corner
Searing silk.

I am the layer of
Dust on a
Poisoned book.

I deal in distortion:
Voices reverse
In me. I speak

Through shadows
Live in echoes
Feed on both

Kinds of oblivion:
Love. Death. They
Couple in my kiss.

Performance is all.
Juggler of
Memento mori

I gore silence
Dip my hands
In it gleefully.

Smother candles
Squeeze night's throat
To vomit diamonds.

My breath is close
Smells of sweetmeats
And dry earth.

I grin across the ages
Moon's skull in
A clouded sky.

Sisters of the Grange
buried alive A.D. 989

Faces pressed
Up through my shoes
As battlefields
Reclaimed by moor
And wooded graves
Petition those who
Cannot mourn.

Stone walls
Three feet and
A body deep.
Maggots fed on
More than mortar
Crawled into the
Cracks of cries.

Wanton weeds and
Faithless daisies
Gossiped between
Paving slabs
But did not hint at
Accusations or suggest
The scent of death.

The garden's dark
Vow of silence
Was not broken
Though feet trod
Upon the pathway
Seven lonely
Women long.

Outside the aisles
Wimpled flowers
Briefly bowed
Subservient heads.
The silence swaddled
Flawed madonnas
Invoking Mary Magdalen.

You lay so long
Without complaining
Labouring beneath
The stone. Now others
Fight new silence
Walling children
Yet unborn.

Kites Abbey

The end of a cart track fronted by woods.
Now, only the name remains – and the ground
You chose when you built your house. No kites fly.
Other birds are irreverent in the trees
Where childless women with uneasy eyes
Journeyed between enclosed walls and the sky –
Will power instead of wings. Those women wept
Yet kept faith: time of praying has ended.

The words they once carved on the tree are lost
And you grew wiser – enough to accept
The well's depth without trying to drain it.
Will never mourn the kites' former soaring –
Long wings less distinct than their forked feathers.

The American Bar

Saturday night in the American sector.
A few lonely faces at empty tables
Bespectacled boys with short hair and Stetsons
Plucking the gingham cloths with thin fingers.
And the rest of the tables over-heavy
With whooping GIs and Berlin women
Shrieking for burgers and Southern Comfort.

Joe tries to pull his sweat-shirt over his stomach
And stretches to put on another record.
Between the tables and the bar they shuffle
Along the edges of a clumsy square dance.
Mothered by kisses and manicured hands:
New York, Kentucky, L.A. – hemming in
A square of stained floor-boards in West Berlin.

Mrs Mackie

Thor's a netty in the kitchen
Ahint that door: waal's a bit femma.
Roond heyor, most fowk
Gan in the yard – cistin is
Alwis freezin' up and ye cud
Breck yor neck on them stairs
Oot the back – twenty-fower –
Aa coonted them mesel
Day w' moved in. Had te lug
The dressor up wiv a rope.
Wad he' smashed te smithereens
If the lads doonstairs
Hadn't ev held it. Me man's muthor's –
Dark oak – a deed weight
Aa've alwis hoovered roond it.
Divvent knaa hoo aa'll tyek it oot.
Sh' shud've put w' in
A proper bathroom
But sh' knaaed sh'd nivvor
Get owt back on the rent.
Just shut the door
When ye de yor dinnor.
The front winder wants a shove
Sash is brokken, but the road's
Ower mucky anyways
And the buses myek it rattle.
Divvent gan an faall
Doon the stairs – oil-cloth's ripped.
If the sink clogs up, nivvor worry
It gans doon slaa lyke.
Aa's not keen te gan ye knaa
Divvent think it.
If aa cud get aroond
Withoot this soddin' frame
Ye waddent hev a chance
Of a playce lyke this.

ON INDEPENDENCE
AND RESOLUTION

The Peepshow Girl

Amongst the long grass
Of down-town Berlin
Manet settles
Behind shutter five
And begins to sketch.

She flexes her back,
Turns on a stare.
Other shutters shoot up.
She rotates – her back
Curved to Picasso

She knows that Degas
Is watching her legs.
Coins fall through the slots
The shutters shoot up
For a minute; clatter down.

Her limbs drift through postures
The minutes fall.
She will leave fully clothed –
A throng already gathering
For the next session –

Take the U-Bahn with tourists,
Schoolboys out after hours,
The unmarriageable, the deserted,
The curious street artist –
Disquieting them with avid eyes.

September 1943

Dear _ _ _ _ _ _ _

The trains help the night keep time; marking certain minutes past
And on the hour. My dreams align with them, rushing the dark.
Locked in our different compartments with empty carriages
Between us – we do not meet. I see us hurtling through
The bombed remains of cities. Each station a gaping hole
Where the platform dropped away; where the train can never stop.

There were no windows in the truck which you were forced to board
While they brought me on here by road with the other women
To these lines of squat huts where we work or lie and listen
To the trains entering the tunnels of our sleeping heads.
Each night is spent trying to roll the heavy door across
And run back down the track, hoping to find you before light.

Morning swoops down: gold on its talons. Clawing up new sounds
To drown the noise of trains. They make us clap back the shutters,
Strip us of our dreams. My rough hands cling to keep them draped here
Across these windows glaring starkly over empty beds.
There is an ache behind my eyes when I put my weight to
The unyielding door, and feel only the creak of the sky.

Years ago, in another country, I saw an eagle
Fly between two mountains, its wings sweeping gold on the sea.
My father put aside our old troubles and exulted:
'They that wait upon the Lord shall renew their strength; they shall
Mount up with wings as eagles; shall run and not be weary.'
Lately, I have heard his voice more clearly; just as I wake.

Owl Woman

The woods hide rough nests – explosives, arms.
I wrapped myself in his coat and lay down.
The birds forgot me: rabbits came to graze
In the early hours, as far as the houses.

Through the new estates eyes turned back
Behind gagged windows. I slept in leaves:
Damp hands lifting lint; a draughty ward.
Branches conferred too low to catch words;
My stained clothes stank. He wrote,
'They have taken off the other leg.'

Owls called in darkness, a distant ache –
Weighing me up, rocking swivel heads
Like the doctor, craning, inquisitive.
My widow's peak, a skull cap;
Black olive eyes, segmented face.
My head, hinged back smooth halves
Of a tawny fruit. My nib of a beak.

'Put your hands on the holes in my head
Feel where my legs…' I cannot move
But watch him. Slow shutters blink.
We need each other for definition.
He stares into the sky. I see nothing,
But he spies birds who veer off
Before they reach my vision.

Your beak opens and you stretch,
Draw yourself in, taking breath –
I move my hands down to feel
The ridges of your feathers.

Tethera

Yan, tan, tethera, methera
CUMBRIAN SHEPHERD COUNT

Always the third sheep to be counted.
They came struggling out of the water,
Shook themselves like huge dogs on the beach,
Ignored our fires and took to the hills
As that first wreck swept under the waves:
Screams are the same in any language.
For many shapes of the moon the sea
Washed ashore men's bodies. We left them
In the shallow caves then moved inland.
Sea – a thin blue line from the mountain
When low clouds pass. We did not go back.

Sheep graze slate-lined streets: steady workers –
The persistent rasp of savaged grass
Has come to soothe us. They move heads down,
Their backs like dirty leftover snow.
Wool nests collect, blow into gullies.
New lambs squeeze in between the tree roots,
Heads wedged against the trunk, out of the wind
Which chartered this city; set statutes
For a shepherd people who see life
Always at an angle; whose stories
Fell from damp fleeces heavy with weed.

Swifts flit in and out where the mountain
Allowed our forefathers to enter.
We gather crooked spires of foxgloves,
Strip leaves to make the heart beat faster,
Start a pulse beaten by the weather.
Most valleys now think us legend.
Down there a cow walks across a field
Surprisingly quickly, smaller than
A brown bead of dung. We feel rain nip.
Change will come with their disenchantment,
Bringing them here – yan, tan, tethera
Eager to mate with our daughters and sons.

Father Lofts Retires

It was not lightly done to sacrifice
People for the small-talk of flowers;
Count purlins and rafters swelling with rain;
To sleep in a house starting to grow again.
Creeping branches had lifted gutters;
Ivy made its way through the walls,
And the earth oozed with unknown wells.

Ashamed, he did not miss parishioners' feet
On the hollow stairs, or the vast back room
Where he took his meals. There was more life
In the squabbling birds, and sheep
Occasionally raising a senile cheer,
Than he had ever known in the gaunt manse
With its curtains falling on bended knee.

Pheasants

The colour of paths: a dull, speckled brown.
I watched her cross the gravel by the door;
Circumnavigate the lawn, breast-high in grass.
A dowdy bird with the wind up her skirts,
Lifting fans of feathers as she strutted –
Out on her own as the air shook with rain.

In green balaclava and red face mask
Her mate invaded through a hole in the hedge.
Rain glistened on his copper, black-ribbed back;
On the metallic tan of breast and tail –
Tipped upright in the wind, like a hat.
A chauvinist bird (in the modern sense)

He insisted on following her around –
Half-raising her wings to the daffodils
She hid among the flowers' yellow heads
While he peered, parrot-like. At last she fled
But froze in her tracks at his harsh, throaty cry
And turned back as if resigned to her lot.

Then, freedom meant to the end of the hedge
Or a few minutes by the magnolia tree.
Two days later, she was hit by a car
And died more dramatically than she lived –
Since when, he has paced this short lane – nagged
By her new independence, and more rain.

Second Honeymoon

Only one of us arrived at the old hotel.
Madame unlocked the door to stale air,
Apologetic walls. Alone, my tightly fitting toe
Teased the slight tear in a damp sheet
Among corridors of vacated rooms
Window bills murmuring *A Vendre.*

Rain made the dining room a candled cave.
Maids draped with coats ran to bring brooms
And swilled it through the aisles into the street.
At another stranded table a woman sat
Dressed for herself, reading a book,
Absorbed in the place's tender despair.

The top storey shutters were battened down.
No one seemed to come or go, yet there was
A light at the top of the stairs
As if someone was quietly remembering
Cars cruising in, a volley of corks, the din –
White cloths piled high with fruits de mer.

In the night the sea rolled up over the road
Whipping pebbles at windscreens, chipping wings.
This morning, below the peeling shutters,
Cars seem shocked, gritted with gravel, barnacles
On their salt-stained tyres; seaweed exhausts.
Severed tentacles smear the lobby floor.

Today the light rings silver, off-key.
Madame sits by the door with tightly clenched fists
While men she might once have invited in
Shoulder heirlooms past her tired legs.
The road is strewn with shells and hollow crabs:
I cross a livid tidemark; scattered sand.

Anniversary

This morning I felt the same recklessness
My marriage-morning fostered years ago.
Then, I walked barefoot across the garden
In my grandmother's crumpled yellow silk,
Touching each damp rose or the squeaking grass
As if determined never to forget –
Now, my older feet bear traces of sand
Up the white-painted stairs from my small room
To this wide bed where I have slept alone
Hearing the wind toss spray against the glass.

I walked out to the dunes before day broke.
It seemed that the turf sprang over new graves:
The ones I have taken so long to dig.
They all lie there now – the grief, the guilt;
No more than a rough carpet for my feet.
And after twenty years I think of you
Putting aside the yellow silk, as if
You knew you must memorise my limbs,
The way they fell on the sand-scattered bed –
Before others should cause you to forget.

Candles

We burn them for love – a man on Skye poured
The purple of the mountains into sand
Near a narrow loch visited by whales.
Beyond three rowan trees the sea grew tame
And nightly he would light the floating dark.

Beside the bed, this pool of wax in sand
Melts walls to make an island estuary.
New tides rib the sheets; damp bodies poured
Relax the skin of mountains, taut before
The warm loch lured the leviathan.

Guardians

The roses will be heavy now at Foxhill;
They bear the house down towards the lake
And the vast rooms where we used to live
Will stare as sunlight hesitates.

I remember the sound of the bird trapped
To flap all night in the panelled room,
How bats and stars sparkled in the stained glass
And windows flew open in the rain.

The swans will come back to nest and feed,
Children litter the lawn with their debris
And from this far garden I have decreed
New lovers to gather on the fallen tree.

Obsession

Days pass as dreams: he never wakes
From the rattle of the needle –
Day after day he sews vast wings.
Josepha squeezes between bales
Of tough white sail-cloth as she sings.

Meals come on a reach – up the stairs:
He stitches panels into place.
Her arm, a boom across his thoughts,
Thrusts down the tray. Her oiled black hair
Swings like a rope out of his grasp.

She makes him polish brown-grained knees,
Her white blouse ripples from beneath.
He notices her feet are wet
Starts to take stock of her veneer
Is stopped – and does what she suggests.

He plays her hair out through his hands
Watches her artful practised arch.
She smiles – he strokes her varnished legs;
Sighs – he will turn away from land
And haul the white blouse to her neck.

On Independence and Resolution

The man next door snores in Portuguese.
He keeps me awake all night, then doesn't speak
When he hands me your letter in the morning.
What would be the point? I could only smile
Like a door closing quietly, if he did.

Bells drag their shadows across the sand
To a glimmer of children. You will not know
The pain I feel when I read her name
Mentioned carelessly, so many times.
I will wish you both well and send my love.

Some nights I dream of what led me here; how I feared
The woman who walked up a road to a shuttered house.
I love the wind chimes of rigging in the harbour:
When the tide comes in, the sea is always warmer;
And your smile does not curve into a key.

Ghosts

In her dream she woke as usual,
The bed felt softer than she remembered
Her head did not turn easily
And something was sitting on her feet
But this ceased to worry her.
The room felt full of people.

It often happened in this house –
Usually they didn't stay too long
Sometimes didn't properly form
But she preferred it when they did.
Ghosts with faces were more
Interesting. They had faces now.

They had surprised her at times
Where she least expected them
But in all these years
Had never come into this room
Till now. These seemed quite
Different. More substantial.

She found their macabre eyes
Disconcerting. They seemed
To hover round the bed.
She was sure they were talking.
Though she had sensed conversation
They had never spoken before.

They were moving closer. Becoming
Clearer. She did not know them.
Their faces swivelled.
One drew the curtain.
Another lifted the sheet
To her face.

Marion Lomax was born in Newcastle in 1953, grew up in North-umberland, and now lives in Berkshire. She gained her doctorate from the University of York in 1983, and her study of Elizabethan and Jacobean drama, *Stage Images and Traditions: Shakespeare to Ford*, was published by Cambridge University Press in 1987.

In 1981 she received an Eric Gregory Award, and won joint first prize in the Cheltenham Festival Poetry Competition. She was Creative Writing Fellow at the University of Reading in 1987-88, and has lectured in English at St Mary's College, Strawberry Hill, since 1987.

The Peepshow Girl is her first book of poems.